In a Dayz

PART 1

JOSHUA GOVANS

Fulton Books
Meadville, PA

Published by Fulton Books 2024

ISBN 979-8-88505-487-4 (paperback)
ISBN 979-8-88505-488-1 (digital)

Printed in the United States of America

PART 1

In 1992, it was estimated that 135,687,063 babies were born throughout the world. Approximately 370,730 babies were born on November 8 in 1992. In that year, it was the 313th day of 1992, in fact it was Sunday at that. The next same calendar year would land in the year 2020 which I am currently writing this in. There is currently eighty-four days until my next birthday that falls on Sunday for the second time. It will be the forty-fifth Sunday of 2020 like it was in 1992.

I started writing this on my 10,140th day since birth. According to statistics, I have spent 3,381 days asleep (9.26 years). I've technically spent 33 percent of my life asleep, having 344 full moons since then. Speaking of sleeping, when I was 6,361 days old, I had a dream that changed my life. You can say mostly my way of thinking. But back to the days, in all these days I have spent in this place, I have noticed one main thing. The past controls this place that we all commonly call earth.

At first it crossed my mind as of course, but the more I put more days into that thought, I find a deeper meaning behind it. A meaning that could be thrown away as easy as the wind blowing a piece of paper out of your hand, but on the other hand, it could have as much weight of the earth itself. As I am writing this now, and I think that it is truly in the eyes, no, in the mind of the observer.

I wish it could be easy enough to fit in a few sentences, but I know without complete understanding, there is no way to justly sum up an observation of something on such a wide scale. A mere analysis is subjected to time. In order to observe anything, we need a start and an end point. Meaning in order for us to give an observation of anything, we have to observe it over time, which creates our starting point until we find an endpoint. There are some things that we would probably need an eternity to come to a conclusion, which is hard to fathom how long that would take. Sometimes there are things that are just impossible to prove.

As a kid, I used to have a thought that would drift around my head from time to time. The thought, "What if everything I am experiencing is a simulation? How can I prove there is consciousness outside of my own?" I know as I'm writing this I chuckle to myself, but nonetheless, I still haven't thought of a way to prove this.

On this earth, we share this common ground where our mind influences the world around us. To break it down, we all come with two realities. There is one that we all share on this earth, and the one that we create with our mind, and both of these do exist. The funny thing about our minds is that it can't tell the two apart at times. For example, dreams, but it's not limited to just that. We also experience daydreaming as well with our eyes wide open. The point I'm getting to is that our mind's reality can be molded by this world constructed around us. And when I say *can,* I mean *it is,* and also vice versa.

Now whether you choose to believe, that is truly up to you. But if you go throughout history and records. You will notice that these people that helped inspire the future all started from a mindset. And from their mindset, they influenced the world they all shared. Most of us are not aware of how much influence our minds have on this earth. For example, our daily lives are shaped from our thoughts and decisions, which can also affect other people's lives and thoughts. Now this all can be proven by science. Wow, let's reverse engineer that, and we can also use this influence to the science. I am not a whistleblower. I am not the savior. I am just an observer.

In order for me to consider something a fact, I first run the new information with the information I already know. If it runs congruent with each other, then I accept the new information as a fact. As a safety precaution, all of the information that I have obtained or stumbled upon is fact until proven false.

If it cannot be proven through this world that we all share, or it doesn't make sense through the information that I am already aware of, I consider it false until proven otherwise.

Nothing is set in stone because there is constant discoveries and information coming out every day. To leave information set in stone, regardless of evidence in my eyes, is foolish and arrogant. Or even the idea to stand behind and even fight for ideologies you don't understand, let alone explain the science behind a theory, is primitive to me. It's the equivalent to the view of nonreligious people on religion, to blindly follow something they can't see or prove exists.

On the contrary, most of those who put their beliefs in science are in the same boat. If they can't come to the same conclusion of the theory on their own accord or if I go to tell you that you can walk on water, are you going to blindly believe me or go test this theory yourself? The two main things that this world revolves around are science and religion. These are two things that you can only prove depending on your beliefs/methods of how this world works and its creation.

As I look at the world, I see a miracle or blessing, whatever you choose to call it. Either way it's here today where we have spent all of our days. All of these different views are what obscure our vision of what and how we perceive things. Most of the things we know are based off an observation of someone else that we can either relate to or not. We ourselves believe in things that we personally can't prove or willingly accept the ideology that has already been set in place. This isn't me saying that everything we know is false. I'm only stating that it is a possibility. A part of me can't just willingly accept all as truth without proof behind it.

GOVERNMENT

As a society, I see us all as sheep. Now I'll explain this opinion. Since we have been confined by the laws of the land, we all share a similar view or structure in thinking. Before we do something, we think of others and how they will perceive our actions. Not only how others will perceive it, but also how it is perceived by the laws of the land. We have also put the power of decision over our lives into another group's hands. I choose to say group because those people, who we have gave or relinquished the power to, do not come from the same level of living that we do. Meaning they do not undergo the same struggles that we share as the people. We are all caught up in a system that has a reset button anytime you start making it out, and a downward spiral for those who are struggling to stay in the same spot.

As I view this system that was set up before me, I can't help but see a huge disadvantage it holds over the people. Let's think about this… So from my understanding, at the end of the chain or at the top of a company is a millionaire/billionaire who is telling us to work for them, and in return they will pay us, correct? While we as the people accepted their offer with a belief that we could achieve what they have accomplished like they did? I would have to say if not, then why would we agree to such terms? Ask yourself, what millionaire do you know worked a nine to five their whole life and made them a millionaire till this day?

I'm pretty sure not one person will pop in your mind, yet we still choose to let them tell us how much our time is worth. The more I look at it, the more I'm dumbfounded that this is still going on today. To abide by a system that makes us, as the people, work hours that consume our days and our life for people who spend possibly no time on the same company we are slaving for, while they make millions to live their life barely working. We are caught in a system that pays a certain amount to the low class, that makes it so you can't afford to miss a day of work and groomed us to believe this is a way of life.

These struggles that we face that the other group does not, most people in power do not survive paycheck to paycheck. They are well set with enough money to buy them out of most problems and situation, let alone be bribed by the people who have generational wealth or wealth in general. So to put it simply, those who we have entrusted with how we live and to make sure there is equality and someone to govern the government on our behalf have been compromised. And it's not just recently we have seen this all over history of revolutions and movements that made way for a genuine change within a nation, kingdom, village, or town. From what I see is they have programed the people to settle for less and less over the years of history they leave for us to perceive. In this current year 2020, I have seen it the most and at a rapid speed that I have never witnessed before.

We should also keep in mind that these same individuals control what we can and can't know. Meaning they can deem information too overwhelming to inform to the masses. In other words, we are limited, as a people, with knowledge to back if it is the whole truth or not. One of our main resources for obtaining knowledge is the internet. Nowadays, we have the power of a library and more in the palm of our hands. Yet, we still have limitations on that as well. Have you ever gone to YouTube or any social platform, and have seen a message stating, "Sorry you are unable to view this video in your country?" That sounds like restricting information that is on a public server, and also public knowledge to some. I guess where I am getting at is how you gauge information to be too overwhelming. Are there some sort of guidelines or scale system in place to help with this?

I believe that if we cannot get a change from those in control, then within our rights, we individually should see fit on how to make one.

GENERATIONAL DIFFERENCES

To divide and conquer is to split the people—from big to small, dark and light, and mainly young and the old.

As we dive into the aspects of time, I want to stop by the topic of generations and their differences. I will start my view with the advancements of technology, and its effects on human to human, let alone human interactions. But that isn't the only thing that it would affect. It would also affect the efforts and the way hard labor would be carried out.

If we start in the 1900s, automobiles, airplanes, and the radio was just being introduced into modern life of America. Now before the car was introduced, we would use horses, mules, or some form of beast for the carriage to be pulled. That was their main source of transportation at that time other than by train. We can also assume the same for farming or any other forms of labor. Now as we create more inventions that make human labor obsolete, we create a subconscious view that humans are obsolete or just an operator.

To start on the topic of generational differences, it will take some explaining, so please be patient with me. Let's start with a view that every generation observed the world at different times. We can take three time periods as an example, the '80s, '90s, and early 2000's. In each one of these time periods, the world was in a different state in time.

The '80s were when we started advancing in technology. We developed disposable cameras, personal computers, compact disks, and more. This was also the era of blockbuster movies, and the roll out of early cable networks like MTV and many more. MTV alone gave a boost to music videos that would soon boost our consumption of music. We also had many now-outdated slang terms like, bodacious, gnarly, tubular, eat my shorts, and radical—terms that would shortly fade out toward the beginning of the '90s. This period of time was also when the crack epidemic first hit the streets of the US, and guns illegally being put into communities.

Now the '90s gave birth to the rising internet, that in turn, gave way for more forms of communication to broaden its methods not only communication but also radically effecting business and entertainment as well. This is also the period of where the rap genre would reach being the most common genre on billboards. The '90s, just like the '80s, had numerous slang words ranging from *don't have a cow* to *the bank's closed*. This was also the era when fast food reached even bigger heights in its industry.

The early 2000s opened up with a terrorist attack on 9/11 back in 2001. We also went through a recession, the stock market crashing, and many more events. This is when skinny jeans became the new fashion, iPod touches were rolling out. Also camera phones became available commercially. This was also the generation where YouTube and Facebook went online. We also had the USB drives, Bluetooth, iPhone, and smartphones within this generation.

Now what may seem like a bunch of random information holds a lot of important details. The one obvious thing is that no generation was the same in almost any way. Another thing that you can take notice of is that technology has made some quantum leaps in progress. We witness trends come and go like the seasons, and problems erupting within every generation. One major thing I realize is that there is always something new, whether it's a trend, a new form of technology, or a form of plight. It is natural to see in the world around us. Nothing stays the same. But in this instance, this is more controlled, I believe.

Before I get into that, all generations will have their own methods of doing things for obvious reasons. One may sit down and read a book while the other reads books on their tablet or iPad. This goes for the newspaper vs the websites and etc. Insignificant it may seem, but this makes it so they have a controlled or instinctual reaction or process.

To give a small example, let's use math. Since the '80s, math has come a long way. A lot of methods have been deemed outdated or completely removed from the curriculum, and this is the same with every generation. So the '80s way for completing a math problem would completely differ from the early 2000s. Our methods have changed so much, that if we gathered those three generations, and have them use scrap paper to show their work, most likely all of those papers would show different methods to obtain the same answer for the most part.

If someone who grew up in the '80s has a baby in the '90s, by the time their child starts learning their mathematic skills, it would be almost impossible for the parent who went to school in the '80s to assist with their learning process. Schools are teaching different methods to solve problems every year or so it seems.

Textbooks are changing right along with everything else. I truly wonder how many times we revised and changed our history books since the '80s alone. Either way how I see it is what we have now is a whole bunch of scattered information. that has been deemed truth at a period of time, then false in the next. Now if this is not the case, I'm just wondering what's the reason for all the new editions.

Now that you may have a better understanding of how impactful generational differences are, I can now start to go into more details of how this may be in importance to us as the people. What we have obtained is a gap between each other starting with our ages. It is natural that not everyone could be born at the same time, but this creates a gap as a people with no bridge. Without this bridge, how could we, as a people, correctly support and teach each other without any miscommunication?

Now I'm going to go into how I perceive this system's methods and goals. I believe they found this method while using capitalism, and seeing that they could preset what's in, when it will be out, and what to replace it with. To me each generation, in other words, are test subjects and are used to gather data on reactions, trends, and popularity. Then after gathering the information, it is used to further whatever agenda they have in mind. I started to have an idea on how they target their audience or chosen market.

If you take a step back and look at how trends and certain markets are targeted, you get a better understanding of their methods. Some of the trends may be, for example, during the lockdown, toilet paper was one of the most trending items over most in the store, only due to the pandemic of course. But also look at how effected the markets are during certain times. As I look at that statement, I think to myself, "Wow, that could be used down to the science" which to me is a possibility. We can go throughout history and see what problems made which industry do well in that time period and made others do worse or close in some cases.

After enough situations and scenarios, businesses and owners could hope for or assist certain scenarios to happen for huge profit gains. They have a market to target each and every generation, ranging from kids to the elderly. One could even stop to think, "Well why have one for kids if they can't buy in the markets" but they are the influence, so the parents do. We are all subjected to being a part of their targeted audience, the main reason being we are the consumer. If we, as the people, don't buy into a market, that market crashes and vice versa. I believe as long as these generational differences affect us, we will all surely fall for everything and anything.

I have an example. Who remembers when the tide pod challenge was going viral? First thing is, if there is such a deadly/dangerous trend happening, why not sensor or shut down such platforms that allow it? Any who, just as easily as that happened, I bet money that their stocks went up, but then went down. It went up because of the trend, and possibly from negative results, it went down due to less people buying it. These markets are more controllable than we perceive that they are.

I know, to be in the section of generational difference, why I'm talking about the markets so much. To answer your question, since we have established these markets, they have impacted and influenced all generations at some point of time. It could have been the reason a business closed, someone lost a job, or even pricing of housing and more. These markets are the very reason why prices are what they are and fluctuate how they do. They control the very power of our dollar or any form of currency at that.

Now back to being a targeted consumer, it had to start somewhere, right? So I started to think, "Okay, so when was I first targeted?" But I couldn't think of it. I never looked at it from that perspective as a child. Note that one thing I remembered is that I wanted everything, whether it was flashy, colorful, unique, the list could go on. I just kept thinking, and one day it dawned on me when I was watching TV with someone. They target us from around six months and up—from what we watch to the message in the TV shows and movies, all the way down to the toys and clothes we want to play with and wear. By the time five years went by, we have become successfully groomed by the markets. From there we are guided by what's popular and what's recommended.

The earlier we are brought into the market, the easier for them to guide each generation in a controlled manner. If you ask me what the main increment would be, I would say ten years. But there are some sub timeframes that would break into two and five years as well. To put it plain and simple, we all have been targeted from a young age until now. I like to call it herding. We have made it so whatever is put in our face, we accept it, and whatever direction that is told, we go. That is down to our decisions made on eating, and all the way down to how we should politically think.

HOW THE PAST CONTROLS
THE FUTURE

In order to fully rap your mind around this, you have to admit that you can't truly prove something happened if you didn't exist.

Let's use a disconnected standpoint, just an open idea to that everything we know. We can't prove based off our knowledge if it was in the past before our existence. Adopt this thought if you will, "If a person controls the past, they can control the future." I know some of your first thoughts are: How can somebody control the past? And if so, how could they control the future?

My thoughts are if they're in our present, it's possible. Someone from the past can't control the future, only influence it. And someone from the future can't change the past, only learn from it. But there is something about the present that is almost magical, something that seems like it never changes on us.

Maybe a good way to describe it is when you are in the middle of a task or activity that you enjoy, and you can't believe that you didn't realize the amount of time that passed. No, more like something that we can all relate to; it's more like when you reflect on a memory, when you think on a moment of your life. The only difference is that you're now imagining that moment. But in that moment, it gave off the same feeling as the present is moving right now. This magical feeling of the present never changes. That's why we say it feels like it was yesterday when I was twenty-one. I believe it feels like that because that magical moment of the present doesn't change, only the things that we are experiencing in that change.

Now with this realization, let's dive back into the "If a person controls the past, they can control the future." Now for this, I am going back some years. Let's say knowledge is power, which I'm pretty sure a high percentage would agree with me. So if we view that as a truth, imagine if there was knowledge one hundred or two hundred years ago. Just for headaches that would be 36,500 or 73,000 days ago, depending on which timelapse you choose. But if a family was the only one with this knowledge, then that family could have power or control of the knowledge that flows congruent with the magical present, which could make a huge difference especially if that knowledge could impact your life in a positive or constructive way. Then that could make a huge impact on history or even the future itself.

My thoughts on this is that the information depends on the severity of the situation. Now I may receive backlash, criticism, and negative feedback from my next example. I stumbled upon a letter from Willy Lynch written in 1712. Now this letter was an informational and instructional writing on how to successfully "tame" the black man or African Americans. This is only a slight example of how this ideology was used against an ethnicity.

Now compared to the history of man, that wasn't too long ago. To be realistic, to me, it would be arguably comparable to saying in the life span of humans as a whole, one could compare the time span being equivalent to a week ago. Now imagine if that same letter was sent out to every slave. Do you believe they would have had the same results? I would disagree.

Half of the mind games that were used to keep them at bay would have fallen short due to their awareness of their situation. I believe they wouldn't have successfully created the feud between a house slave and a field slave simply because they would have had the knowledge to understand it was a deliberate plan to separate a nation from its roots in all aspects and ways. To be honest, you can see the concept in the slave trade entirely.

You have a group of people that I would assume came from just about the same nation, ethnicity, and possibly religious background. You take those group of people, and remove them from their land, but not only out of their land. They also had their native tongue stripped away from them and also their writing for those who could. They were also threatened to have their tongues cut out if they were caught speaking (any language) or have their hands and fingers cut off if caught writing.

So at this point, their past is now cut off to them, and risk genocide if disregarded. They are no longer aware of their own history, their own triumphs, their own failures, and what makes them essentially *them* in this world with so much history. With all that said, if you control the history, you can control the future.

PART 2

What inspired this piece of work is the thought of looking at everything in the world with a biased opinion. In a sense, it is like viewing the world from a child's point of view, to disconnect with ideologies that are already set in place, and look at things from a face value perspective. This may be a hard thing for some to do so. It's to drop all obligations of what you thought you know or knew, and instead look at it as if you still have to find out.

We tend to let people think for us, even if we can't make sense of what is being said or thought. We try our hardest to hold on to what makes sense to us, or even what makes sense to everyone else. Look at Einstein. He was a man with an extraordinary way of thinking. He didn't come into this world as the great genius he is now known as. He went through scrutiny, ridicule, and much more. He had to fight for the view we have on him now. He had teachers telling him he's wrong, kicking him out of class, or not even accepting him into the school. You could even say the whole world was against him at that point. Only he knew he was correct at the time which I find as proof that just because the masses or important people approve of something, doesn't mean that is 100 percent correct.

How can so many people be proven wrong by one person? This question is a huge one for me. Years of study, some even spending a lifetime were all still proven false in the short time period that Einstein spent figuring out all of his theories. It's hard to believe that we only listen to people who have doctrines, etc. to prove they know what they are talking about. In my theory, that's no proof. That's only a slight idea of their success rate of being correct. To me the only thing that that proves is the time and dedication they put into it. Anybody can see a right or wrong answer. That all depends if they think they know what they're looking for, or if they are just looking to find anything.

Sometimes we go looking for something specific, and cannot find what we are looking for because we are limiting ourselves. We could be looking right at the answer, but since we think we know what we are looking for, we miss the answer that is presenting itself. I'm not here looking for who's right or who's wrong.

From my time here, I noticed that we all bicker over "Who's right, who's wrong, what's right, what's wrong." From what I see, we now have gotten to the point that people don't care about what's right, just about being right. I believe that is what Einstein was going through during his struggle. He wasn't just fighting to prove his theories. He was fighting people's prides and egos. How could you spend so much time and research just to be proven wrong by a mere student?

In my thoughts, they must not be the greatest teacher only because a true teacher is always a student. Even if they teach for a living, you can always learn something new. That thought process right there is one of the main reasons why I have a hard time considering a lot that is documented or known as fact to actually be one. We as humans come with emotions and feelings that can get in the way of logical thinking. In a world where it is ruled by ego, pride, and arrogance, we can have the right answer presented in front of us but still choose to deem it false for bias reasons. To me that's the equivalent of saying that facts are based and catered to our mental stability. If that is the case, how could I consider most information presented as fact?

CONCEPT OF TIME

Time is a tricky thing; I like to believe it is only real to those it effects. Not saying that it's not real just irrelevant to somethings or instances, that's beside the point. Time, as we know, flows in one direction. We have broken time into segments and measurements—from milliseconds, seconds, minutes, hours, days, years, etc. We use these to organize this thing we call life.

The most important measurement to me is days. The reason why I say this is because it separates each moment from the last. For example, if you go off a second or minute, it would be hard to distinguish each moment from the last. But with days, you have hours and minutes to help show the difference of what took place in that time period. We also have phenomena that help tell the difference from day and night, plus our natural cycle of sleep that seems like a reset button. Time is tricky because it almost seems like it doesn't exist, similar to the wind, without its physical presence on this reality, like the wind blowing the leaves, and the wrinkles time wipes on our face.

As I think and dwell more into the thought of time, I realize how much of a vast topic it truly is, how irrelevant we want to make it, or how important we think it is. I think it is safe to say it is useful. I would even argue important at times. Now it may not actually gauge our maturity, but it does give us a base understanding of how long we have occupied our common ground called earth. I view some aspects of time equivalent to the chapters in a book. It is designed to separate or distinguish events or phenomena that has taken place in different time periods. Now this method is used from history, all the way down to how scientist conduct their studies and base their results.

GENETICS

I would like to take the time to sit down and explain my thoughts and views on genetics. I have not sat down and have done excessive amounts of research on this topic, so it won't be a long one—one that is shorter and to the point. And with that being said, I believe that our genetics are always changing ever so slightly, nothing that can be obvious but still makes a difference.

I believe the things that slightly alter it especially how nowadays are. Our food and drinks that we consume, and drugs and alcohol, I believe, have a huge impact on our DNA as well as the climate. Whatever we do in repetition and simply anything physically or mentally presented to us in are life in abundance. Now with this being stated, when it comes to the reproduction part of DNA, I have observed that most people when they are born resemble their parents. I know what an obvious analysis, but when I state that, I mean an exact copy of the parents at that very moment in time.

You are free to judge with this example, but I'd rather you understand fully than to leave it to the individual to assume what I mean. So with that being said, if a male were to preserve his semen and the same with a women and their egg, I believe if they choose to conceive a child with the preserved egg or semen, it would resemble the parent at that age and time. And if they were to have another child a year later with their current DNA, the child would resemble them at the time of conception.

So when you look at the children when they get older, pull out an old photo album that you had or check out Facebook or other social media. You will notice that the kids may have certain facial features or expressions that are unique to that time period. It doesn't just stop there. It also could be behavior, thought processes, and more unique details. Nonetheless, it would be proof that our DNA alters or changes over time. But then again, I have never setup an experiment or have tried to gather evidence of this analysis.

A THOUGHT PROCESS

One of the vastest things known to man, a mind, one can argue that statement with the very universe itself. But who can even prove the vast amount of space in each one? It's almost like looking at a computer chip and guessing how much gigabytes it can hold off of the mere size especially now that our technology is growing at an alarming rate with no sign of slowing down. But that's for another section.

The point I'm making is how can you gauge or measure how vast a person's mind is? It comes with so many functions on top of having its own autopilot features. We can breathe, talk, blink, walk, and eat all at the same time. We should give it more credit than what the average joe does. I could spend all day complimenting the brain and all of its achievements it has and gained over the years.

We, as a conscious being, have come along way. We have built off the last man's ideas, thoughts, and words whether that's further proving some-body's thoughts or ideas, to even proving someone's thoughts or ideas are false. We have built a mental or a conscious empire with everything as a whole that we have accomplished. It's truly outstanding and remarkable, a world wonder in itself. What led me to touch this topic is the strength in the topic alone. "A Thought Process," a strength that is constantly undermined.

The more I think about it, the more I think of thoughts like the very ether itself that could make something out of nothing. Our minds are put so low that we look outward for entertainment, strength, satisfactory, comfort, reliance, and love when all of this stuff can be found in our own mind. In society we are almost programmed to have others thinking for us which in our beginning stages are normal because we lack the common sense that we gain over time. But in our case, you can say we are treated like it never existed.

We constantly have everything screaming at us on what to say, do, think, feel, etc. while we are perfectly capable of doing so. How is that, you may ask. Well, I can throw out a few examples. Let's start with advertisements. Nowadays, they're everywhere. Technology only helped solidify their heavy presence that is here today. We, as the people, rely on technology almost like we do oxygen which molds us in the smallest ways like knowing simple math, and calculators make it so it's not a necessity. We openly dull our mind like having something read out loud without it being a convenience. For now, I will stop bashing the nullification of our mind and start describing or discussing what I think about a thought process.

I had a friend ask me, "What do you think the fourth dimension is?" To be honest, I can't remember my reply. I just remember him answering, "Your mind." As he was pointing to his temple while we were driving. When he said this, I was lost in thought. To me it seemed true.

We can explore the depths of the ocean, the vastness of space, every square mile of land, yet we can't explore the inner workings of a mind. To even imagine what it would look like in action is a sight I'd pay for. I imagine a formless gas with electrical currents, pulsing in and out of it, that shoot throughout the rest of the body until it makes it out. I know some of y'all are thinking "until it makes it out?" Yes.

Have you ever heard of manifestation or the law of attraction? Well this is an ideology that if you think it and believe it. It will be it or manifest and come true. Now if this is the case, then how I described how I pictured the thought process working would make some sense, but I know *some* doesn't cut it.

So let's break it down from a scientific outlook. From my understanding, everything vibrates, correct? Even at the molecular level, things are always moving. Well what do they say? Our mind operates off brain waves, and this is how they measure brain activity. You know the funny thing about it is that from my understanding, all of these things that we cannot see with the naked eye move in waves and depending on the length of the wave determines its speed and strength. The shorter the wave the stronger and faster it is. The longer the wave is, the weaker and slower it is.

Now with that being said, there are soundwaves (radios and even the noise that comes out of our mouth). I am also taught light travels in the same fashion. The only thing different about these things for the most part are their wavelengths, but they all follow the same rules and principles. Now sound-waves, light rays (waves), anything in its likeness for the most part can pass through solid objects. Let's bring this logic back to a brainwave. I believe they can do the same thing.

So back to when I said that it will pulse until it makes it out. The law of attraction works like when you think it, believe it, then receive it. Well if these thoughts of yours are echoing out of your mind and body, you are sending that into the universe and God, who is always listening. From there it takes your brainwaves and sends you back what you want through the physical.

Now you can look at it like it's a fairytale or a movie scene, but things happen that we don't notice or can't see. If we couldn't feel the wind blow across our skin, I wonder what we would think that phe-nomena was when we see leaves being blown around with no knowledge of a wind current. We can com-pare that to the soundwaves, light waves, and brain-waves; none of these things can be seen, but we still believe it exists. So with that being said, the idea of law of attraction isn't that too far-fetched.

Think of it, have you ever been walking along the sidewalk and see a raised panel, and think to your-self, *Watch me trip over it.* Sure enough when the time comes, you do. Well I believe it's because we only do what we think. Sounds obvious, but I mean every part of it. Think about it, when you wake up in the morning you get clothes ready you take a shower, get dressed, grab something to eat, and run out the door. There's one thing we forgot, brushing our teeth. Now this may not always be the case, but it happens. The part I'm getting at is well why didn't we, it's because we weren't thinking of it at the time.

Our thoughts decide what our whole life is going to be, and what we expect from it. Our minds are more powerful than the computers we use, but we dull it with too many forms of nullification to mention. Also remember in my "how the past controls the future" section. If you can control the mind, you control the people.

With all that being said, think for yourself, first and foremost, and give your mind some more credit. It may seem like such a little thing, but a thought could be just as powerful as an atom bomb, or it can be a dimly lit candle.

DREAMS

So I have a little self-made theory on this subject about dreams. I have adopted the thought that a dream is your soul speaking to you. In order for you to get a full understanding, I will have to first explain my thoughts on what our soul is to us. Our soul is our true essence of who we are, meaning what we were, are, and will be. Our soul is eternal something like energy, it can't be created nor destroyed. In other words, it lives on forever.

It has already lived in every moment of our human experience. Like I said in the time section, *time is only relevant to those it affects.* Meaning time only effects our mind and body but not our soul. With that being said, I believe our soul tries to communicate with us constantly, whether it's a gut feeling, a random idea, whatever it decides to speak through. Dreams are our strongest line of communication depending on the person. So short and simple, your dreams can be the language of the soul, a piece of the true you that's giving you direction, insight, or comfort. Whatever your soul is trying to tell you, it most likely has to do with your well-being physical, mentally, and in some cases, spiritually.

But it can also be your conscious depending on how well trained it is, then that is when you can now control them or even choose to let them act on their own accord. I choose to come back to the subject on another time. I will end it with something I read: Some believe that the dreaming state is the actual waking moment, and we are asleep (dreaming) when we are awake.

DÉJÀ VU

Now this topic is a very interesting one, something that is damn near impossible to understand—déjà vu. This phenomenon is a 100 percent one of a kind feeling. Most of the time, it will leave you in a state of confusion because you're trying your hardest to remember where you have seen this similar reality that you can recall step by step as it's happening.

Now before I came to the conclusion of what this phenomenon is, I was at a complete lost. I couldn't think of one thing that reminds me of the feeling or even something similar. It took me years of thinking to come to this conclusion. Now with this explanation, if you have not already covered my sections on dreaming, I would advise you to go start there before continuing this segment.

With that being said, isn't it funny that when you have a dream, for the most part, it seems real as reality, in our waking moments. Until you wake up and this feeling of a false reality takes in place when you recall the dream, it will shortly disappear from your memory the more attention you pay to the waking world.

So what I did one day—and I couldn't tell you why or what inspired this thought process—was that I compared the feeling of waking up to the feeling of déjà vu. Afterward, I found a striking similarity in both phenomena. They both gave a hazy realistic feeling that's hard to recall the origin or details of the familiarity of the realities.

My beliefs are when you are experiencing déjà vu, you are actually recalling a dream that has happened but has long been forgotten. Now when this happened to me after realizing what I'm experiencing, it would seem as if a mental film or a picture is overlapping the view or event. Almost like taking a picture with a camera and when the picture is taken, it becomes a moment frozen in time.

So anytime you see that picture, you can recall the moment from your memory, and it gives you a realistic recall on the moment. Long story short, déjà vu is you recalling a dream of a moment that is now happening, and that feeling of confusion is you trying to find where you've seen this from. The simple answer which sounds oddly sarcastic is in your dreams, and if you didn't carry that memory with you until that very moment, déjà vu will always be a mysterious and odd phenomenon.

Now for those who want a further explanation on how everything ties in if dreams can be messages from your soul, let's just assume that this theory is correct, and if so, your soul lives forever. Meaning time doesn't truly apply to it. It's always going to exist no matter how long eternity is. Time is only relevant to the bodies our souls occupy because we all have an expiration date when it comes to our physical vessels we experience *life* in.

To put it into perspective, let's first imagine a line that never ends—no start or end points; only a continuous line—that represents the timeline of a soul. Now below that line, let's put another line. Now this one represents our physical body's timeline that has a start and endpoint. Now what these two lines represent is your soul's timeline which is endless, and your body's time line which is limited. I believe that there is a small bridge in between these two lines that connect them, should you say the third line. Now this third line's purpose is to transfer information from your soul to your body or mind in the physical. This connection can come in many forms, but I believe its strongest form is through dreams.

What this mechanism does is send over important information that is detrimental to your health or well-being. So your soul which has already experienced this phenomenon called *life* only tries to assist and persuade your thoughts, decisions, and actions for the better of your well-being. Now whether you listen, pay attention, let alone recognize when it speaks, that could be for another book or special edition if wanted, but I believe there are ways for us to hone in on this. One of the major keys are being aware.

PART 3

So now that you have a deeper understanding of what inspired this piece of writing to come into existence, it is more of the mind expressing its experience in the perspective from the outside looking in. This wasn't made to argue against any theory or to say any theory or idea is correct or incorrect but only to express the idea of open thought. Now this idea of open thought would be to better explain it. It is the thought without worldly guidance. To observe what you're seeing with your own knowledge and not running it by the world's knowledge of what it is already known for.

We can find ourselves trying to think for others, or even have others thinking for us. The funny thing about that is there are some things that are only true pertaining to that person. I've heard of this saying that "everybody is right." It's a weird concept, but I find some truth to this. I personally find it acknowledging the mind's world that I mentioned in Part 1. It removes the world we share and takes a look at the one that is only known to us. It's almost like saying that whatever you believe is true, just maybe from only your perspective, but nonetheless it is a truth to at least one person.

I would like to call the truths that are true due only to perspectives as personal truths. I believe there are universal truths and conditional truths. Meaning there are some truths that are true in every situation and scenario given while there are other truths that are only true under certain situations and instances, or even a personal truth. When we take the time to break those down and look at them separately, it gives us a different perspective of what we are looking at.

TV (TELEVISION) EFFECTS

What brought me to this subject is the undeniable influence that it has to the individual while effecting the masses as a whole. I would like to start this subject of topic with, "monkey see, monkey do". This will be my personal thoughts on the effects of television to the normal person. Where I am choosing to start is daily consumption; how long does the average American watch TV throughout the day?

According to Statista, the average American spends at least four hours a day watching tv. I know that doesn't sound too bad. Until you add in your eight-hour workday, and then you start to notice how much time you give your brain to just think and act on its own. I personally believe that the average American watches more TV than four hours.

My personal belief is that we consume anywhere from four to six hours on average with a high being eight hours. We all have our shows that we can be fanatics about, but do we ever stop to think if this is a good thing. Yea it's a great way to pass the time, but that's not always the case nowadays. Now it's a part of our daily routine.

I hope you don't mind if I ironically say *daily programming*. TV is one of the most important things in our society before the cell phones came into play. The television soon started to consume every aspect of our life that could be thought of. It went from a source of information or news, to entertainment of all sorts and varieties. Could you imagine if for some reason, there were no more things to watch on TV, not even reruns? Many people will become depressed, in a sense of disarray. Some even angered from the sudden change.

There will be a small percentage where there will be a positive change in. The few that it doesn't tear down will help strengthen their connection with others, first off. Not only that, but they will also soon realize that they can entertain each other like we did for thousands of years.

I believe the television could be used for a positive outcome, but what we are currently witnessing is the negatives in it. What I have observed is that slowly over time, we start to insert more and more negative things that we would rarely see in person in our daily lives. Maybe not insert but allow such negative things to make it onto the big screen.

One example is murder. Depending on where you live, that is not something you see every day unless you work in a field that involves that. I believe that over time, what that does is nullifies our emotion and reaction to murders. I would say in some cases, we do not want to watch a movie or a TV show if it doesn't have enough in it. So we have developed the opposite of what our true nature or morality is. We can find every act that we punish or shun in our films and TV shows, and we look forward to it.

Now I know we understand that it is just TV. It's all acting, and I agree. The only thing I have a hard time agreeing with is that it doesn't have an effect on us. Not only that, but what if there are also individuals who those acts resonate with? That could take a turn for the worst, depending on what they resonate with. We should keep in mind that just about anything can be aired on our screens, except for explicit material. The odd thing is that we still do but in a more controlled fashion that isn't as explicit, but yet we still try to come as close as we can. Not only that, but we also have very loose restrictions on preventing our young to witness these scenes and TV shows. So not only do we have to worry about the effects of explicit material on the adult mind, but also the juvenile's minds that have easy access to the material.

If you still haven't reached a part of my conclusion then I will say, to me, there is no question why we have high crime and also violent crimes. I like to believe that if we have never seen something, it most likely wouldn't happen or come to existence. For example, imagine trying to explain what colors are or even describe one to someone who was born blind. Do you think they would be able to get a correct image of what you're describing? Of course, the idea isn't fool-proof.

The proof of that is in art or even in inventions, they had to create the idea within their mind or be influenced by something they have seen or been through. Long story short, most of our problems are still a problem because we put a spotlight on them in every chance we can. For example, we have crime shows. We also have the news that delivers our bad news along with (pointless) good news. Now we have programs that air live stream feeds of police cams and built a whole TV program around it. It doesn't stop there. We also have prison shows and more. How I see it is that there's two or more views that can be made from that. You have the encouragement of becoming an officer. On the other hand, it encourages people into crime or glorifying prison life.

We as the people have a hard time seeing this because it's more of a subconscious deal we consciously view as entertainment while our minds can perceive it how it wants. What the TV does is expose us to all kinds of scenarios and situations that we most likely would never be in or witness. That could also be thought of influencing good or bad. We as humans only do what we think. If we don't think to do it, we simply don't. In other words, I believe the TV is a tool to provoke targeted thoughts and thought processes. With that being said, influence is almost impossible to get around. It is the building blocks to our progression as a person and species.

BRAIN WASH

The reason I included this topic is only due to the effects that television programming has on the masses, let alone an individual. I believe that our powerful brain can be manipulated so effortlessly if we allow it to be.

Our brains are like a sponge. They absorb any information that is accessible to them, good or bad. The strange thing about the brain is that it never truly forgets anything. In a sense, you can say it is turned into a compressed file that your subconscious can simply find and or locate. We remember symbols, sounds, textures, and more.

The thing about this is like I mentioned before, our brain can't tell the difference between a thought or a real-life event which kind of furthers my point that our brains can be easily manipulated. Meaning, if we see the same things over and over again and hear the same things over again, one, we won't forget it; two we have a large possibility of believing it. Not only that, but if a large group of our population agrees or believes something as fact, we all will also eventually fall in-line and start believing the same thing not because we actually see it and recognize it as a truth but more because we see others doing so.

Now whatever the reason maybe, eventually we will start to recognize it as a truth. There are many different methods that are used to achieve the same results. We as the people may have a hard time believing that at some point, we have been brainwashed in some form or fashion. We as the people also have to recognize that, this could be taking place right in our very face. If we cannot recognize it as that, it would simply be whatever they are presenting it as. That could range from anything like school, TV, work, videogames, and more.

I'm sure the list could go on the more I put more time into thought, but these are things that wouldn't ring an alarm. Not saying it should unless it's true. We have studied our humanistic behaviors so much that we couldn't overlook how influential we are which would lead them to the next thing that would be hard to overlook, that is, how controllable we are. We are programmable, in other words. We can be placed or forced into a habit and will naturally adjust to it so much to the point that we will convince ourselves that it's good or for the better. In my opinion, the individual will benefit more if they are able to keep their own opinion separate and/or in mind when dealing with outside influences.

HUMAN BEHAVIORS

Humans, such a fascinating thing. One of the most complicated but yet simplest things. We are comprised of emotions, logical thinking, and self-awareness that trickle down into habits, instincts, and perception.

We come with a hive mind mentality but still hold on to our individuality. We all, whether we are aware of it or not, are habitual beings. Meaning repetition consumes a lot of our lives from the moment we are born. We all live and learn through repetition. Surely, we all do not succeed everything on our first try. I'm sure our parents can attest to that. We had to try and crawl and walk plenty of times before we were successful.

It reminds me of the term I heard of called the ten thousand-hour rule. What this term represents is that anything you do for ten thousand hours essentially, you become a master at it. I tend to hold a lot of truth in that only because I have seen it with my own eyes while also accomplishing it myself with a couple of skills. I mention all of this because this is the first thing we all have in common. We all learn/learned from the same process. We all are a lot more alike than we would probably want to credit or acknowledge. We all have basic reactions, instincts, and processes that are ingrained in every one of us.

What brings us our individuality is our own personal experiences that we go through. To bring into perspective, most of us would have the same reaction or response to the exact same scenario or experiences. If we all lived the same life, going through the same experiences, we would find very little difference in character between us.

I will provide an example of how we share similar instincts that could remind you of a hive mind. Let's say we are walking down a busy street in New York. You have trucks blocking lanes to unload or pick up merchandise, multiple conversations going on around you. Cars are probably honking, loud music coming from them, people walking in almost every direction. Then all of a sudden, everything is moving in the same direction, conversations have ceased, and panic sets in place. It's a mass hysteria, and the only thing that isn't is the direction that everyone is moving.

Now logically, would you run against the crowd or would you run with them? I'm pretty sure I don't have to answer that for us to assume the correct answer. It's instinct even if we think different now. We will most likely run with them. Now this is just one of so many habits, reactions, processes, instincts, etc. We as a species can't hide from this just like mostly every other species on this planet. We are capable of being aware of this process with ourselves, and a fairly easy task to recognize it in other species. We have created time periods based off other species for example, spring and fall. That's what led me to this thought process.

We all have something that can trigger us to have the same reaction. We all have the same triggers in the direst situations unless you have been trained or exposed to the situation on multiple occasions. The hive mind is something that we aren't too aware of only because it's like second nature to us. We don't realize that we tend to follow other people's path or ideas. If we don't know how to get to a place, we will try to find someone who's going to the same place. If they say there is a nation-wide food shortage, people will go out with urgency to get themselves their food, no matter the cost.

Now that's with or without money, our survival instincts would kick in. We tend to rather have people think for us than anything else. Unless it's a survival setting then we are driven to think for our self. Outside of that, we look to others for our decisions, our livelihood, and even security. Whether that's mental or physical, we tend to do whatever the masses approve of. We tend to go off of group thinking mainly because that was our best tactic at surviving at one point of time which I believe is engraved in our genetics. It's a natural thing for us to have.

In my eyes, we have a slight advantage over our other inhabitants of this earth. That advantage is our capability to be aware of one's self. I know it doesn't sound like a huge advantage or maybe not a significant capability. This is one of our greatest feats known to man. Some will argue even to the known universe. The reason is because this shows that we can have constructed thoughts. In return we can retain events, think on why or how it happened, and the key point, learn from it. We have the ability to raise our own awareness not only about ourselves but also the things around us.

We are able to construct ideas and bring them from the mental into the physical. In other words, we can create an idea of something and manifest it through our reality. As long as it's within the possibility that governs the world, aka all the "scientific laws."

TECHNOLOGY

Technology became a man's best friend, removing the fluffy K9 that previously held that title. I will try my best not to ramble about this vast topic, but there is much to be covered. I will start with the progression of technology and make my way to my thoughts and beliefs on it. As a species, our first tools were technically our first technology then our wheel came into existence sometime after. Over time, our tools would change as our understanding of our resources and materials expanded. We would eventually move from the stone age to the iron age, and so on and so forth toward more recent times.

There are a lot of things and tasks that we rely on, ranging from all kinds of technology that we rely on to help carry out. As of late, we are heavily being groomed to it whether that's fresh out the womb or months to a year after. For the elderly, they have no choice but to get familiar with the internet if they are not already. Not to mention apps that have managed to takeover any and every smart device. One can even argue that technology is the very reason why we haven't evolved, but that's for another time.

We have started to rely on technology so much that if it were to go away, surely we as humans would take a massive hit because of our modern way of living has been pampering us. We no longer grow and gather food for ourselves, let alone possess the knowledge to. Don't get me wrong, our achievements are impressive, but could also possibly be our biggest setback in the future.

We used animals to do a lot of our hard work, which we eventually replaced with machines. Now most of those animals are now only useful as a food source, while most are going instinct mainly because of technology. These small replacements are all across the board, ranging from starting a fire (lighters) to gathering water. There are many ways to do both, but we have simplified it with no to little prior knowledge of before the simplifications. If there were no TVs, we would have to travel to the next town to hear what happened there. Things would drastically change in a world that has lost its technology.

Now I would like to take a look at where our future is heading with our technological boom. We have so much at our fingertips, we have crossed boundaries that we have once thought impossible. We have flown from continent to continent, and sailed coast to coast. We have turned many processes that could take months or years and halved those times. We have made drones that need no human pilots and are still able to fly with the control of a hummingbird or even better. I won't be surprised when they start the first commercialized flying cars.

We may be a few years, some could say decades, out but with AI prototypes rolling out in 2022, I have no doubts that flying cars won't be so far-fetched within the upcoming years. To some, it may be obvious, but technology is the future. We even built our own new currency based from it (cryptocurrency).

I believe we will reach a point where regular jobs will be discontinued due to our advancement in technology. One example is janitorial duties. Eventually, I believe, we will have robotics to cover every aspect of cleaning. In my belief, the only reason why it hasn't happened yet is due to the lack of duties that are able to be performed. Think about it, we already have little machines that vacuums the carpet on a scheduled basis for homes. We soon, like our animal counterparts, will be pushed out of a job soon due to technology.

I also want to cover Artificial Intelligence (AI). I find this topic very interesting on what the outcome from AIs will be. We have seen in many movies with AIs going crazy and trying to exterminate humankind which isn't surprising to me, but I will get to that situation later. Let's try and look at what exactly this all means. Artificial intelligence itself sums up its meaning with its name. It is an intelligence which some may argue having a mind that we have created artificially. There are series of programs and more that help make it what it is. I would say the goal of it is to see how human we can make our robotic counterpart. Are we able to give an inanimate object the capability to think, let alone learn and have emotions just like us? There are many positives that can come from this new development, but it also comes with some negative possibilities. I will start with the positives and slowly work our way to the negatives.

The positives on having AI technology can be astounding if successful. We would virtually have a computer mind with the capability of learning like humans. We would be able to let the AIs do the thinking for us. We have somewhat already achieved this accomplishment through the self-driving cars. They are equipped with cameras and sensors to calculate their actions while driving. Eventually, this will be spread to everything—lawn mowers, vacuums, and eventually databases. Soon we will be able to give it a formula, problem, or a goal, and it will search all known possibilities until it reaches a conclusion which will be most likely faster than having an whole team of humans working on it due to the information that can be available.

I believe, soon, we will put an AI in the internet, if we haven't already, to obtain all the information from it. With that it will be able to learn the history of humans and how we are as a whole through our interactions with the internet (mainly social networks). In a positive way, this could be used in many ways to benefit us. It could possibly gather data on what would work or fit better in our life. It could possibly even figure out how to have us to come together as a species to better ourselves. There are many possibilities on how AI could benefit our livelihood.

Now the negatives on AI may sound a little dark, but nonetheless could still be a possibility. One of the main things I know it will pick up on is that we are a very destructive species. If placed or hooked up to the internet, it will have access to all of our history. I'm sure I don't need to be a historian to realize that our history is filled with conflicts ranging from greed, arrogance, ego, etc.

All of those things can easily paint a picture of how the human race can be. It could also look at the state of the current world and compare the changes of our history until now. Also, if this AI is able to think for itself and understand that it is a new inhabitant on this earth, that could create some interesting scenarios. If it resembles anything of its human counterpart, it could have its own mechanism if anything threatens its existence called self-preservation.

In a world where the mindset "If I'm going down, then their going down with me" exists in a lot of its inhabitant, that could be a threat to the AI if it hasn't already created its way out of that situation. Not only that, but we should also hope that it doesn't look at us as animals like we did. If so, we could have a reverse effect of having the AI claiming dominant species if it chooses to add itself to that category. If you ask me, my opinion is that we are trying to play God, and this can backfire on us horribly. We are trying to make a creation and give it the same gift we received, a consciousness.

PART 4

You know what a scary thing is? The scary thing is a system that is built to have people listen no matter what. You want to know what the even scarier thing is? It is the people listening to one person by their own choice. Now this isn't scary to the people for the one that the people listen to, but scary to the people who are already in control.

It is human nature to follow something, and as humans, it is human nature to want people to follow you or something that you created. Part of me believes that's why most of the world's religions were created. We can all find this in ourselves to have a satisfaction of people liking or following us. Even if it's indirectly through an idea, opinion, or even a creation of some sort. I have a hard time putting it against humans.

SOCIETY WITHOUT CURRENCY

Now could you imagine a society without currency? Sounds like either an apocalypse or some kind of utopia. This original thought was inspired by the thought of a utopia but with that thought came the opposite as well. Almost like a reminder of duality that anything can be done two ways or more for better or worse. Because without currency, there's either a bartering system in place or something of that like the government.

Just because it sounds more amusing, I will start with the apocalyptic sounding scenario. If there was no currency to help guide society, things would quickly turn into mayhem and chaos. It would turn into a dog-eat-dog world where everybody is only looking after their self with no disregard to anyone else. This world that is already competitive and shares the same likeness would only grow more into its ways.

The poor will now adopt the ideology that the rich currently have, which is to obtain as much as possible through any means necessary without any means of helping others. Now the poor would adopt this survival instinct should you say, which leads you to ask, "I wonder what's different about this ideology and our current day society?" The people would no longer be satisfied with what will sustain them, and now look at everything as a limited resource which creates a higher demand mentally for whatever is needed. The world as we know it would regress into pointless wars and battles, which would never be solved due to the lack of compromising and resources.

Well I find it ironic that when you look at this situation and compare it to how the world is, or responds to those same circumstances. You start to see that our responses or reactions are not much different. Nonetheless in these times, most would not resort to bartering, which would lead to robbing and stealing and would only plunge the world more in turmoil. This is a sad truth, but that is what lies in our true nature. It is a safety mechanism. Studies would reveal that it is in our genetics, some can even say its genetic programming and or a development through our genetics, a thing we would like to call self-preservation.

As society starts to become a little more civil again, we would leave such barbaric ways, and start to head toward something similar to the feudal era. To provide a little insight, this era was mostly known in Asia. It was when men with enough resources and power could, in a sense, bully less fortunate people to work for them in exchange for food, housing, protection, etc. Without guidance in a society without currency, in my opinion, we would surely make no progress as the human race.

Now onto the idea of society running without currency. I understand that this may be one of the hardest concepts to grasp. How is it possible for us to still get everything done, not have the world plunge into chaos and still be able to advance ourselves?

I personally do not believe that every working individual has to work an eight-hour workday or anything past that. I believe there is more than enough people for the work that we have available. In my opinion, I think that everybody could live life working a two to four-hour day, and that should be able to provide them with everything they need. So I have taken certain approaches and looked through different perspectives to view the possibilities within this idea.

The first thing we would have to examine is the amount of work available. Let's start with the US. According to Statista's website in 2020, there were nearly 150 million jobs in the United States. According to the federal census, there were 330,222,422 people living in the USA. Now when you break down the numbers, there is double the amount of people then there are jobs, which I believe furthers my point. I understand that not every job is a job for everyone, but out of all the extra hands we have, I don't believe it would be hard to find qualifying candidates.

What helps drive this façade is that we don't have enough work is to keep opportunities controlled and in a competitive state. Not only that, but jobs are also limited because of qualifications that we as the people have to pay for. Now if you look at this situation logically, if it was a crisis, wouldn't the employers pay for the education or certifications? The sad truth is no. In current society, we have achieved in making a system where it is based off the individual and not the masses. For example, it is possible for one person to own a company and create all the rules or regulations that are seen fit by the owner. It sounds justified, but when broken down, it leads to corruption.

Let us look at this, most things will be put in place where the employed are dangerously dependent on their employer. The sad part is that the deeper you go into that concept, the more you see it in most of the businesses/organizations. This concept can be found anywhere from the corporate world to the government. So in order to fix this current set up, we would have to eliminate all selfish gain from businesses and corporations, so we can transition into more of a community gain objective.

So now back to the currency-less society. In order for us to have a community gain without paying the individual some form of currency, we would have to come up with a system that is beneficial to everyone. As of right now, we are heavily influenced by consumerism. What this does is have us buying products out of want, instead a need or necessity. This current format makes it so we will allow somebody to exhaust all of their resources even if it will leave them in a worse position financially.

So the next step we would need to take to having a successful currency free society is to come up with an exchange for the work done, which is a hard thing to do. We are trying to figure out what can be an actual compensation for a person's time. Something that can never be refunded back or remotely in our control. In my opinion, time is the most valuable thing that humans have because of the limited amount we have. In my opinion, it could be worth everything and that thought helped answer my question on compensation. Literally everything.

I know it sounds impossible or like an ignorant answer. So I will go more into detail about this solution. For example, currently, we spend our time working for money so we can buy the things we want or need. So I have come up with the idea that all you need to do is work, and you are granted or even guaranteed what you need. Think of the old saying "time is money," it is only true because money exists, and we have shaped our world around it.

Before we went to currency, there was a bartering system, to anybody who isn't familiar with the term. It is a system where individuals trade or exchange goods and services for other goods and services. It was a simplistic method that isn't far as controlling as the current system we have set up. This is the system that I slightly based mine off, also accompanied with the current system we are living in as well.

As I'm thinking on how to put this into words, I'm noticing that the idea seems kind of far-fetched, almost like I'm describing some sort of utopia. Nonetheless, it may just be that, or it can be just another form of a civilized society. Now with just the bare minimum of what I have said, some can already see the possibility in this while some are still skeptical of it, which is completely fine. Not everybody will agree on an idea that only one person finds right or possible. We have seen this throughout history. To wrap everything I stated together, if we abolished the use of currency, we could set up a system that provides you with all of your needs for a fraction of your time spent at work.

In other words, there would be enough people where we could work two to four hours of work daily, with the rest of our day to do whatever. In return the government or company pays for your living expenses, all the way down to the car you need to get there. Gas stations would no longer charge for fuel because free transportation is key to a currency-free society. If the government was to provide everything for the people, and in return, the people help build and upkeep their nation, many problems would be solved.

For example, there would be no high class and low class. This system would abolish such ideologies from existing. You would be able to get rid of corruption due to the lack of self-empowerment. In this form of society, the masses work for each other instead of the masses working for a small group of individuals or a single individual. To me this is how the human race should be. It would reflect an ant hill and how they work. How can ants get so much needed work done without a currency set in place to keep order? The idea of being selfless or limiting the chances of selfishness and its acts.

The ants work night and day to serve the queen, or you can even say for the other ants. Surely one ant on its own will not outlive the colony alone, and surely no colony would be that if they all stood alone. They all work to feed each other since they hatched. They have watched other ants tend to their needs. As they mature and are able to take on tasks of their own, they will tend to the needs of the colony. The only thing that could mess up their natural flow of unison is something that gives them a chance to survival as an individual. When I view an ant colony, I believe in looking at a natural system that humans originally started with.

When you look at the Native Americans or early tribes, they started with providing for each other instead of oneself. In other words, if one starves, they all do, and if one eats, they all do. I have taken these views and systems to help produce the system and thought of it being possible. My ideology could be comparably similar with some modern updates.

Instead of focusing on a town or village, I can envision this across the world. I believe as a race or species, whatever you would like to call us, we are capable of this on a global scale. One of the many reasons that is preventing this from being a reality are greed and capitalism. Capitalism is one of the major things fighting its very existence.

I will do my best to give a more detail explanation on how this is possible.

Even if this was possible to become a reality, the current elites and powers of the world would not let this happen. You can say this ideology threatens their control, power, and way of living. I will give a couple examples, so you can have a deeper understanding of the circumstances. The powers at hand completely rely on a society with currency, which should be self-explanatory.

To help bring it in to perspective, a trillionaire can afford to pay everybody in the *world* $140. I know doesn't seem like it can amount up to the stimulus checks we receive, but nonetheless, that is an astounding feat to be able to do on your own. With that kind of wealth, I would have a hard time wanting to make society no longer run by currency too.

I believe with that kind of wealth, they would get rid of anyone threatening their wealth. Not only would the wealthiest disapprove of this system but also some of the middle class. Thanks to capitalism, most will want to hold on to what they have since they have worked for it, some who have worked their whole lifetime. A lot of people will have a hard time with people having better or worse jobs, being able to have the same things and potential as them. Our current society has groomed people to be ego-based to judge worth or value by one's occupation or materialistic value. We put the doctor over the custodian, but both jobs are vital to a society. Society couldn't be the same without one of the other, and that goes for any job/position in society.

I personally believe this way of life could produce multiple beneficial outcomes. I will do my best to give a more detailed explanation on how this is possible. I know there are many things that would need to be changed in order for this to work, but I don't believe it's impossible. It will need serious work and dedication to have a positive impact. Not only that, but we would also need a great deal of patience and optimism to make this idea realistic. We have to look very carefully at the detail of our current economic and social structures while also keeping an open mind to all possibilities and solutions.

THE POSITIVES

As much as I would like to dive deeper into this concept, I know myself there are too many details for me to put down as of now. I will do my best to give you an understanding of my idea in a simplified version. I will most likely dedicate this subject matter into a whole entire book in the future.

Now onto the more positive side to having a non-currency society while not having the world plunge into madness without mercy. I know sounds impossible, very well could be impossible, but if so, it is not due to the idea but due to the people. We as humans have come a long way. We have civilized ourselves. We have created phenomenal things. We have built structures to reach the high of highs. We have created and achieved feats of astonishment. We have made accomplishments of all sorts from being able to have a human fly, let alone making it a means of transportation. Then to completely surpass that with successfully reaching outer space, which would then lead us to our moon landing.

Most of these achievements have been made individually or in a small group/agency. So if we have come this far separated, imagine the progress we could make as a whole. Then we wouldn't be hiding data and information from other countries, and instead share all discoveries to further our understanding, and also our technological advances.

The saying "there is strength in numbers" is such a concrete statement to me. If we could have all of the world's leading scientist working on the same task with no hidden data, it would be hard to imagine what problem, equation, or phenomenon we couldn't solve. Things that would take a single country years to figure out could possibly be solved in a matter of months. On a united front, we can achieve the impossible. We could colonize the very space around our planet and more.

There would be no more homeless. If anything, they would only be nomads. We could solve any food shortage and erase the idea of world hunger. On rescuingleftovercuisine.org, their data reflects that there is 162 billion in annual waste. According to google, it was recorded that there was 7.674 billion people living on the earth. I'm pretty sure I won't need to do the math to point out the question on why is there such thing called "world hunger."

I also believe in our current state in society that we are capable of achieving the same feat. We could also put our heads together on figuring out how to reverse global warming, which would lead to less pollution. With that by itself could help our other inhabitants to survive on this earth that we all share.

RACE WARS

This topic is a perspective from hearing the stories not only in America but also in the world. There is proof throughout all of history of racism and race wars terrorizing societies. You can see it in biblical and mythical texts. It can also be found in our not too distant past. We can turn our eyes to the massacre in Germany with the holocaust as well as the massive massacre going on in Africa in the same time period. The names of the two individuals that are to be responsible for these acts of genocides are Adolf Hitler and King Leopold ll. Adolf Hitler's massacre resulted in the genocide of six to seven million Ashkenazi Jew's death. King Leopold was responsible for the massive massacre of ten to fifteen million deaths in the acts of genocide on the African people.

From these two major events, we are able to witness the extent and the effects that these race wars can produce. As I look at history and view some of the battles that have taken place around the world, I can't help but see this a huge influence, and that it's still continuing on into current days. Whether that is in the world, let alone in the same country I am writing this in. As far as in the country I am in, I can't help but to hear or see some form of the news showing the same results. What was mind-boggling to me was that no one else can see it, but if it's not being done to them, it may be harder to identify it for what it is.

This can even be in some cases or scenarios of when it is being done in front of them. I would like to believe this is mostly because of how systematic it really is. If everything seems perfect for you in a system that's always worked for you and your families for generations. It would make it rather hard to believe that there is a flaw in the system, which would lead to a mentality that there must be a flaw in the person or said individuals.

As long as the system is in a controlled manner it can appear that the opportunity is completely open to anybody, but due to the complete control, it can be a completely different scenario. The race war or acts of war has changed its methods of warfare and is now a mental battle that over laces every side, and every side's actions and reaction. What this does in return makes it that someone who isn't aware of the circumstances could be perceived to hold the same views as the system. When in reality, the system produced a false perception on the system but not just the system, the people or the race as well because of a bias and negative view on a specific demography or people. What this creates is a mass confusion among people who could possibly see nothing wrong with another's race but more on the views and actions of others individually.

With more understanding of how the race wars and how their tactics have changed, we are better fit to not fall prey to a war we want no part of. We can now breakdown previous actions and current methods of this system to find a solution to the problem without slipping into a physical race war.

The first step is understanding how it operates. We, as the victim or bystander, can remove ourselves from the tension that is not warranted. That would result in less confusion and more understanding within communities. The second thing to do is to see within the rights that we have within our country to dismantle such systems and powers that can corrupt. If all else fails, we, the people, can come up with a self-reliance system that takes care of our own needs if necessary.

The act of not resulting into violence will help expose the lack of empathy toward such situations that are present. Working within our own means to support and take care of one and another and will show the short comings of the current system in play. We, as the people who do not fall prey to the temptations of the race war, but seek to change the environment for all should prepare to take on the same scrutiny from the aggressors. Join the cause to show we are not disagreeing with a race. We are disagreeing with a mentality and lack of moral ethics. We will then see what it will take, to see what is needed to get a true understanding of the depths that our world swims over, and our choices to change it.

SELF-CONTROL: MENTALLY, EMOTIONALLY, AND PHYSICALLY

Sometimes I'd like to say I feel like my emotions are strong, even my thoughts and thought processes. I can feel at times that an emotion is a different thought process of me. One could even say a different me which I know in layman's terms, people will try to call this schizophrenic, but I don't recognize it as that in this case. I tend to look at it as a dynamic piece of who we all truly are.

So with that being said, it is a piece of our natural person. Some people have a hard time understanding let alone recognizing that. We, as people, all react from emotion whether its directly for something or indirectly. Meaning it effects only what you think and from there we react to our feelings of that emotion.

I have found myself where I am very close to controlling my emotions. That doesn't mean I don't feel them. I only know how to deal/cope with them which in turn gave me an understanding and insight while I was going through them. That is what sparked my very mentioning of this topic or thought process because I would understand and observe my reactions and my feelings while not reacting. I learned that I am observing my raw self come out, and if I couldn't understand it, then it would surely control me.

I would be a slave to impulse, and something in that bothered me. These thoughts and ideologies floated around, forming and shifting new reactions and understanding.

At this point I am rewiring my brain in a sense, or you could say taming it. But it doesn't stop there because you now can remove these emotions or put them to the side and look at things for what they are or could be. The thing that inspired me is that it builds true character within yourself. When you gain control of what you feel like choosing to put emotion in, then you can start building a stronger foundation within yourself.

When I did this, I found myself putting my thoughts and emotions into things that can make a difference and change things in a positive or enlightening manner. I also found that you can transmute emotions and feelings through other emotions or in my standpoint, creativity. Me having a large heart for emotions and feelings leaves me with many wise thoughts from empathy, reflecting/reflection, and an open mind. What this does for us is helping us gain a better understanding of thy self. You are taking the time to look into the mirror and be aware of your actions, feelings, and thoughts. From there you are on a pathway to having a better understanding of not only you but also everything else around you. Granted, this may not work for everyone or be viewed the same. That does not mean anything less or more for these individuals. We all have things we struggle to understand, control, and do. If your are one of the fortunate, use your understanding to help and/or give your contribution to further the progression. Nobody's perfect.

Would you believe me if I said that I get little snippets of a message that I have to write down to see what I'm saying. Or I get images of a small picture, but I have to draw them out and put them together to see what I was looking at.

ABOUT THE AUTHOR

Joshua has always taken a liking to the interesting format of words. Ever since he was young, he would enjoy hearing stories and reading them himself. He grew up in a small town in the tri-state area, where he would spend most of his time. Little did this author know that he would find himself writing books, but it should have been obvious to him. The same kid in middle school, writing short stories and books on ripped up papers with staples to hold it together.

So no wonder by the time high school hit, he found himself reading and working on his comprehension skills. He would spend his times doing physical activities, playing video games, or reading a book. He has always had a mind-blowing imagination, only lacking a descriptive way of describing it. But his love for words would refuse for that to stay the same forever. He loved the expression he was able to relay through writings in all forms of it. Whether that was through storytelling, opinions or thoughts, even down to poetry. We now have a chance to peer into the mind of the author and explore all the inner workings of it and his imaginative marvels of work.